Writers and their Work
A critical and bibliographical series

General Editor
Ian Scott-Kilvert

HORACE WALPOLE
from a portrait of 1754 by J. G. Eccardt
National Portrait Gallery

THE
GOTHIC NOVEL

by

BRENDAN HENNESSY

General Editor
Ian Scott-Kilvert

PUBLISHED FOR
THE BRITISH COUNCIL
BY LONGMAN GROUP LTD

LONGMAN GROUP LTD
Longman House, Burnt Mill, Harlow, Essex

*Associated companies, branches and
representatives throughout the world*

First published 1978
© Brendan Hennessy 1978

*Printed in England by
Bradleys, Reading and London*

ISBN 0 582 01259 7

CONTENTS

THE GOTHIC NOVEL

I. INTRODUCTION

THE DESIRE to be terrified is as much part of human nature as the need to laugh. This has been recognised for as long as stories have been told, and today thriller writers and makers of horror movies depend on it. Popular kinds of novel devoted in predictable and artless ways to curdling the blood of the greatest number are understandably neglected or dismissed by literary critics. But one genre among them, the Gothic novel, which was originated in England by Horace Walpole's *The Castle of Otranto* in 1764, and which flourished until the 1820s, has received much less attention than it deserves.

The term 'Gothic' has three main connotations: barbarous, like the Gothic tribes of the Middle Ages—which is what the Renaissance meant by the word; medieval, with all the associations of castles, knights in armour, and chivalry; and the supernatural, with the associations of the fearful and the unknown and the mysterious.

The Gothic novel was one aspect of a general movement away from classical order in the literature of the eighteenth century, and towards imagination and feeling, a development which ran parallel to the Romantic movement and presents many points of contact with it.

There is justification for the view held by some critics that the Gothic novel was a wrong turning, in the sense that it left the mainstream of the tradition developed by Richardson, Fielding, Smollett and Sterne, and did not find its way back when that tradition continued with Jane Austen, Sir Walter Scott and Dickens. Characterization tended to be sacrificed to the demands of complicated hair-raising plots, and the settings, elements and machinery associated with fear were over-exploited until they became monotonous. The weaker writers also overworked the emotionalism of 'the novel of sentiment' developed by Richardson, to which the Gothic novel was a natural successor. Saintly heroines gushed tears by the bucketful.

No one can deny that it is against the stock, or cliché, responses that, as the critic I. A. Richards put it, 'the artist's internal and external conflicts are fought', and that with them 'the popular writer's triumphs are made'. On the other hand, it is narrow-minded automatically to equate 'popular' with 'hackneyed' or 'bad'. The popular Shakespeare, Dostoyevsky and Dickens possessed the kind of energy that overspilled into excesses: it is at least doubtful whether their geniuses could have been expressed in a more selective way. The best Gothic novelists deserved their popularity, and some still demand to be read. Some were highly individual artists who added much to the scope of the novel. Some exerted a seminal influence on other literary genres.

The Gothic novel, in satisfying the hunger for mystery to replace the certainties of the eighteenth century, awe and fear to replace rationalism, plundered the Middle Ages for its settings, content and machinery. The characters, though they may look medieval, are generally contemporary in thought and speech. Gothic architecture, though in a vague rather than a realistic way, was part of most novelists' settings—in the form of a half-ruined castle or abbey—and was used to create 'Gothic gloom' and sublimity, all those attributes that evoked awe. A castle had fairy-tale as well as medieval associations.

Such buildings displayed all the paraphernalia of fear: dark corridors, secret underground passages, huge clanging doors, dungeons with grilled windows. Nature was picturesque— ivy growing over the ruins and wild flowers in the cracks; and turbulently romantic—dense forests on mountain-sides, thunderstorms. The scene that hauntingly recurs is of large black mysterious birds encircling a castle on a stormy moonlit night, in which owls screech and bats flit about. There are evil doings in the vaults, terrified fugitives stumbling through passages with candles, a weird white-clothed figure glimpsed in a beam of moonlight that is fitfully cast across the ruin of a wall or a cell window, as it shines through the gaps in the thunderclouds.

Various manifestations of the supernatural and of witch-craft recall those found in the ancient classics, and in the Icelandic sagas. The *Iliad* has ghosts, and the Icelandic sagas of the thirteenth century contain many supernatural elements, while the medieval romances, Dante, and Malory's *Morte d'Arthur* (1485) also exerted a powerful influence. But the immediate sources for the Gothic novel's supernatural content, elements and machinery are to be found in Elizabethan literature, from Spenser's fairyland to the portentous visitations depicted in Shakespeare. During the Gothic period the Elizabethan and Jacobean drama was revived, and the more bloodcurdling the better—Webster, Ford, Marston and Tourneur were performed and acclaimed, as well as Shakespeare.

Terror and horror as main ingredients had been plentiful in poetry and drama from the *Oedipus* of Sophocles onwards, but not in the novel. Though terror is used effectively in Smollett's *Ferdinand Count Fathom* (1753), it only provides one or two episodes among many. Witchcraft had been prominent in much literature from Apuleius's *The Golden Ass* (about 170 AD) onwards, and there were many Elizabethan books on the subject, followed by a treatise on demonology written by James I.

The novels to which particular attention has been paid in this essay are those which possess either a seminal importance, notably *Otranto*, or a raw, bleeding vitality and originality which gave them enormous popularity in their time and has kept them alive today—those of Lewis and Maturin for example—in defiance of critics whose palates are perhaps over-delicate.

II. HORACE WALPOLE:
THE CASTLE OF OTRANTO

Horace Walpole, the fourth Earl of Oxford, the youngest son of the statesman Robert Walpole, had a long and productive life, as Member of Parliament for twenty-six years, writer of essays, voluminous correspondence and memoirs, and as an antiquarian with a taste for Gothic architecture. He died in 1797 at the age of eighty. Walpole suffered some ridicule in his own time for the eccentricity of turning his home at Strawberry Hill, Twickenham, near London, into 'a little

Gothic castle', and for the extravagances of his novel *The Castle of Otranto* (1764). He had his champions, but today he and his novel are regarded as curiosities. Here is a widely talented dilettante, who through an accident of literary history created one of the most influential novels ever written. A greatly flawed work, it is hardly readable today for its own sake, but it contains innovations that have inspired numerous imitations and developments.

Walpole's (and the eighteenth century's) ideas about architecture were strongly influenced by the remarkable etchings of the Venetian architect Giovanni Battista Piranesi (1720–78), with their 'sublime visions' and dramatic contrasts of light and shade, exemplified in the series of imaginary prisons, *Carceri d'Invenzione*, and in the views of ancient and modern Rome.

The rooms at Strawberry Hill were, in Walpole's words, 'more the work of fancy than imitation', more Rococo than Gothic. There was a monastic hall with statues of saints in arched windows and a staircase with suits of armour, but much of the decoration was sentimental or quaint. The Gothic Revival, as the architectural and antiquarian movement was named after the early decades of the 18th century, had been separate from the revival of the Gothic in the 'grave-yard' verse of the pre-Romantic poets. But in mid-century there were writers of importance known both in the field of literature and as students of Gothic architecture, such as Thomas Gray, and Kenneth Clark maintains in *The Gothic Revival* that Gray has undeservedly been overshadowed by the attention given to Walpole, and that it was literary taste which influenced the new Gothic architecture rather than the other way round.

However that may be, Walpole's importance in both movements derives from combining extensive antiquarian interests, a desire to revive Gothic architecture, and his liking for the medieval tales of chivalry. All these elements came together in the novel, inspired by a dream of the author's in which he found himself in a castle and saw a gigantic hand in armour at the top of a staircase; the story was then written in a two-month rush.

Even the basic plot, quite apart from the supernatural

elaborations and difficulties in method, cannot be taken seriously today. One has to make a great effort to see it from the standpoint of the age, hungry for magic and mystery after many decades of rationalism.

The setting is Italy. Manfred, the prince of Otranto, a usurper, has arranged the marriage of his son Conrad to Isabella, daughter of the true heir. The evening before the wedding a huge helmet falls on Conrad, killing him, and it is discovered by a peasant, Theodore, that the helmet is like one now missing from a black marble statue of Alfonso the Good, a former prince, in the church of St Nicholas. (A Piranesi etching shows an enormous plumed helmet hanging over tiny men.) Manfred says that he will divorce his wife Hippolita and marry Isabella. At this, the plumes of the helmet shake, the portrait of Manfred's grandfather in the gallery comes to life, sighs, and goes into a chamber.

Isabella escapes from Manfred through an underground passage and is given refuge by Father Jerome at the church of St Nicholas. On the way she has met and fallen in love with Theodore. Matilda, Manfred's daughter, has noticed that Theodore, with his jet black hair, is like the portrait of Alfonso in the gallery, and is also in love with him. Manfred is told by garrulous servants that a giant's leg in armour has been seen in the chamber at the end of the gallery.

Father Jerome is ordered by Manfred to give up Isabella and to behead Theodore, but when the monk discovers that Theodore is his son, the young man is spared. Isabella's father, Frederic, the Marquis of Vicenza, arrives. He is the nearest relative to the last rightful owner Alfonso. An enormous sword, carried by 100 knights, is let fall near the helmet where it cannot be moved. Manfred tries to persuade Frederic that there should be a double wedding—he with Isabella, Frederic with Matilda, Manfred's daughter. Three drops of blood fall from the nose of the statue of Alfonso in protest.

Manfred confesses that his grandfather poisoned Alfonso in the Holy Land, and by a fictitious will the grandfather was declared his heir. Jerome turns out to be Count Falconara. Matilda is killed by her father who in an insane fit of jealousy takes her for Isabella, and the castle is shaken by thunder. The giant Alfonso appears in the middle of the ruins, shouting, 'Behold in Theodore the true heir of Alfonso'. The new prince, Theodore, marries Isabella. Manfred and his wife will spend the rest of their lives in the convent, repenting.

Walpole's aim was to make the supernatural appear natural, especially through the portrayal of characters placed in unusual circumstances. He wanted to evoke all the magic, the marvels and the chivalry of the Middle Ages without losing the reality of his own time: the characters, therefore, although contemporary in thought and speech, were as fully credulous about the supernatural machinery as if they were 11th–12th century people. Sir Walter Scott, strongly influenced by Walpole, pointed out that this was the first 'modern' novel to attempt such an effect, and by calling his work Gothic, Walpole rescued the term from its previous derogatory sense of anything that offended against true taste.

Appreciating that his effort could lead to bathos if not disaster, Walpole treated his work as a half-joke in his first edition, pretending that it was a translation from an old Italian manuscript.

Original as Walpole's concoction was, it was in the peculiar combination of the elements in a new kind of novel that the originality lay, rather than in the elements *per se*. The laws of chivalry, and the saintly hero and heroine came from the old romances, and there are incidents that show Walpole's acquaintance with fairy tales and oriental tales— for example, the servant Bianca rubbing a ring before the giant Alfonso appears is reminiscent of stories in the *Arabian Nights*. There was a restless ghost, Patroclus, in Homer's *Iliad*. The talkative servants derive from Shakespeare's use of them as comic relief in his tragedies.

If not original in detail, Walpole was remarkably inventive. There were three significant innovations in his novel. First, there was the use of the Gothic castle of romance with all its appurtenances as the pivot for the work. All the Gothic machinery is there—vaults, passages, dungeons, convent, gusts of wind, moonlight, groans and clanking of chains—and Walpole in his matter-of-fact way demonstrated its potential. He showed how it could be used in combination with old romance elements, and how ghosts could be given a definite function in the plot. The device of the portrait coming to life is found in many subsequent Gothic novels, notably Maturin's *Melmoth the Wanderer*. So are the devices of feigning translation from an old MS, and such borrowings from old romance as prophecies, dreams and Theodore's birthmark, by which his father recognises him. Mrs Radcliffe and others favoured the restoring of the hereditary rights of their protagonists after they had been cheated, as they were restored to Theodore, and Walpole's use of Italy as a setting was copied by many, for the monks and the horrors of the Inquisition—if they did not prefer to make it Spain.

Secondly, Walpole was innovative in the way he used the forces of nature to produce an atmosphere, to indicate the mystery of life, the possibility of evil forces shaping man's fate. As Isabella hurries through the underground passages, her lamp is blown out by a gust of wind, and the same wind will relentlessly blow out heroines' candles and lamps for many years to come. Moonlight is supposed to add to the awesomeness of the giant Alfonso's appearance, and it will more effectively accompany future ghosts.

Thirdly, Theodore, in his appearance, provides one of the sources of the famed Byronic hero—dark-haired, handsome, melancholy and mysterious. The other characters became the stock characters of Gothic fiction, and once again Walpole pointed to the way they would generally develop, though he did not provide more than sketches—the tyrant, the heroine, the challenger, the monk (there were to be both saintly and evil varieties), and the peasant who turns out to be noble.

The most evident shortcoming in the eyes of the modern reader is that Walpole fails to create an atmosphere of mystery. The pace and clarity that propel the story forward work against mystery, since what is required is some vagueness or obscurity, that would stimulate the reader's imagination. The plot is over-convoluted, and the machinery appears too quickly, one episode crowding upon another, before each has time to take effect. Since the characters lack individuality, the reader is not sufficiently involved. They twist and turn like puppets, bewilderingly gushing tears one moment and declaiming stoic sentiments the next, with

Prince Manfred ('his virtues were always ready to operate, when his passions did not obscure his reason', Walpole says jejunely) adding sudden bouts of callous cruelty. Amusement or irritation is too often the reader's reaction to a scene which is aimed at producing a shudder, so that the illusion rarely displays any power. From Walpole's shortcomings in this sphere Mrs Radcliffe was to learn how to create eeriness and grandeur by setting a slower pace in which the atmosphere has time to build up.

The association of *Otranto* with a dream, and the author's readiness to draw upon the unconscious, together with such magic happenings as the flow of blood from the statue have led to talk of Walpole as 'the first Surrealist novelist'. But it hardly seems necessary to protest so much; absurd as he appears today, sufficient claims have already been made for giving him attention.

III.   WILLIAM BECKFORD: *VATHEK*

The influence of the Oriental upon *Otranto* has been noted. *The Arabian Nights*, which dates from about 800, was translated into French by Antoine Galland in 1704, and other Oriental tales appeared in English at about the same time: more recently there had been such works as Voltaire's *Eastern Tales*. Most of these had been read by the scholarly William Beckford (1759–1844), the author of *Vathek* (1786), an Oriental-Gothic production of great originality. It is about a Caliph who in his hunger for knowledge and power becomes a disciple of Eblis (the Arab version of Satan), commits many horrible crimes and undergoes numerous grotesque adventures before finding eternal torment. Beckford also translated Oriental tales and wrote satires and travel diaries. In these last he also testifies to being strongly affected by Piranesi's etchings, and his descriptions of the ruins of Istakhur, below which lie the infernal regions of Eblis, are undoubtedly a tribute to the Italian architect.

Vathek, being exotic and poetic, on the surface a burlesque of the Oriental tale, with an elegant humour and irony that keeps the terror of its incidents at a distance, was not at first considered Gothic. But subsequent Gothic novels and tales incorporated the fairy-tale exotic as well as terror, and Beckford's combination was highly influential, in both Gothic and Romantic fields.

Like many Gothic writers, Beckford was eccentric. He was set apart both by the great wealth he inherited from his father and by his homosexuality. There was a scandal over his relationship with William Courtenay, the young son of Louisa Beckford. She was married to a cousin of William's, but was in love with the writer and encouraged the relation-ship with her son as a kind of sacrificial offering. Beckford was virtually coerced by his family to travel abroad for several years, and he was ostracized by society when he returned. Later he indulged his taste for the grandiose by building Fonthill Abbey, a gigantic Gothic structure with a central tower 300 feet high, which collapsed in 1800.

Vathek was written very rapidly in French when he was twenty-two, translated by his tutor Samuel Henley, and finally revised by the author. Its composition seems to have been directly inspired by the week of Christmas 1781, which Beckford spent at his luxurious country seat, with Louisa, William Courtenay and the painter Alexander Cozens, who has been suspected of having initiated the writer into magical practices. Beckford never forgot this visit and nearly sixty years later described it in ecstatic terms:

Immured we were . . . for three days following—doors and windows so strictly closed that neither common daylight nor commonplace visitors could get in or even peep in. . . . It was the realisation of romance in all its fervours, in all its extravagance. The delirium into which our young and fervent bosoms were cast by such a combination of seductive influences may be conceived only too easily.

It is the last part of the novel that indelibly impresses itself upon the imagination. Spurred on by the sorceress Carathis, his mother, Vathek has arrived at the subterranean palace of Eblis, where the promise to regale him with the sight of the pre-Adamite sultans' stupendous treasures is to be fulfilled. He is accompanied by four princes and Nouronihar, the daughter of one of his emirs, whom he has abducted on the way. The splendour of the scene is evoked by the use of exact and sensuous detail. There are

.... rows of columns and arcades, which gradually diminished, till they terminated in a point radiant as the sun when he darts his last beams athwart the ocean. The pavement, strewed over with gold dust and saffron, exhaled so subtle an odour as almost overpowered them. They, however, went on, and observed an infinity of censers, in which ambergris and the wood of aloes were continually burning.

The horror is just as stylishly described. A multitude roams through these luxurious surroundings with 'the livid paleness of death', their right hands not leaving their hearts, some in a trance, some 'shrieking with agony', all avoiding each other. Further on, through halls lit by torches and braziers, in a place with long curtains, brocaded with crimson and gold, they enter 'a vast tabernacle hung round with the skins of leopards' in which Eblis is sitting on a globe of fire being adored by multitudes—'a young man, whose noble and regular features seemed to have been tarnished by malignant vapours'. In the gloom of a huge, domed hall are the wasted forms of the pre-Adamite kings, lying with hands covering their hearts, and through the transparent chest of the most renowned Vathek sees the heart in flames. The guide says that after a few days during which they enjoy the sights and are permitted to demand access to all the treasures, Vathek and his companions will suffer the same fate.

They wander in increasing despair through the halls, without appetite for the magnificent banquet laid out, and without curiosity. There is more power here than in most Gothic writers, and it has accumulated in the more light-hearted, earlier scenes in which Vathek prepares for and accomplishes the journey: here Beckford takes us so urbanely into the fantasy that we accept it just as we accept any fairy tale. We smile when people collapse or even die under a darting glance from Vathek's eye, but it is a smile of complicity.

Thus we accept the fate of the fifty boys sacrificed to the Giaour, the Indian who guides Vathek to Eblis. Vathek pushes them one by one over a cliff, at the bottom of which the Giaour is waiting to eat them. (We are, however, glad to learn, much later, that a good Genius saved them.) Carathis makes a sacrifice to the subterranean Genii, piling serpents' oil, mummies, rhinoceros' horns, strongly smelling woods, and 'a thousand other horrible rarities' on top of a tower and setting it alight. We almost admire her expediency when 140 inhabitants of Samarah, the capital city, bring water to the top of the tower. Carathis has them strangled by her servants—a band of mutes and black women—and thrown on top of the pile to make an even bigger sacrifice.

Yet when Carathis arrives, as planned, at the Hall of Eblis, the atmosphere of profound dejection makes her crimes now appear monstrous abominations rather than absurd exaggerations in Voltaire's *Candide* style. We shudder when she explains to Vathek how she has buried his wives alive with the help of her black women, 'who thus spent their last moments greatly to their satisfaction', before setting fire to the tower and destroying them too, together with mutes and serpents. We leave them, together with Nouronihar and the four princes, with hearts on fire, all hating one another, 'in ghastly convulsions', screaming.

The tragic mood of this last episode poignantly suggests a degree of identification with Vathek on the part of Beckford himself. While in earlier scenes the author seems to be standing back from the action, enjoying his creature's iconoclastic antics, and the way he makes fun of the old and the reverent, in the end he no doubt projected some of his own sense of being rejected and isolated, young as he was when writing the novel, into Vathek's fate. Nouronihar, in her submission to Vathek and willingness to follow him into any crime, is another Louisa.

Vathek's message has been convincingly interpreted by his biographer Marc Chadourne, in the light of Jean-Paul Sartre's play *Huis Clos* (*No Exit*), as a parable on the theme that 'Hell is other people'. One man and two women are condemned to live in a prison cell, and each is in love with the person who does not requite the passion. (It reminds you of Mario Praz's comment on the spiral staircases in Piranesi's prisons, leading nowhere: 'anxiety with no possibility of escape is the main theme of the Gothic tales'.) *Vathek's* message, Chadourne says, is that hell is within ourselves as well: that passion is transformed into disgust, love to hate, and that we must say goodbye to all hope. However far we go with Sartre or Beckford in that view, it is certainly the dark side of Beckford which especially appealed to such admirers as Byron (who called *Vathek* his bible), and Edgar Allan Poe.

The writings of Hawthorne, Baudelaire, Meredith, Swinburne, Mallarmé and Wilde can be found along the many trails which lead from *Vathek*. For the moment, it is most relevant to note that in 1815 the poet Percy Shelley and Mary Godwin, his mistress, had been reading it.

IV. MARY SHELLEY: *FRANKENSTEIN*

Beckford talks of Vathek's 'insolent desire to penetrate the secrets of heaven'—in effect he sold his soul to the Devil, and that is a decidedly Gothic motif, to be taken up again later. *Frankenstein* (1818) is the story of a scientist who in creating a human being finds himself responsible for a monster and murderer: it displays strong affinities with *Vathek*, in that the impulse behind it is the desire to show how dangerous can be the attempt to discover the secrets of life. The tale became one of the principal progenitors of science fiction, and the scientist's tragedy is indirectly a criticism of the same 'unnatural' curiosity that the author's husband, the poet, showed in some of his work.

Mary Shelley (1797–1851) derived a marked independence of mind and spirit from her father, William Godwin, the political theorist and author of *Political Justice* (whose belief in the perfectibility of man through reason strongly influenced her husband), and from her mother Mary Wollstonecraft, an ardent fighter for women's rights. Mary Godwin met Shelley when she was seventeen: he left his wife, Harriet, and the pair eloped to Switzerland, marrying in 1816, when Harriet committed suicide, and settling in Italy.

In the summer of 1816 the Shelleys were staying with Byron, his physician Dr John Polidori and Matthew Lewis at a villa near Geneva. Byron read some German ghost stories and suggested they should each write one. Out of this came the first vampire story in English—Goethe had published a vampire work in 1797—Dr Polidori's *The Vampyre*, developed from a sketch by Byron. And Mary Shelley wrote *Frankenstein* after listening to conversations between her husband and Polidori about Erasmus Darwin's theories of evolution, and impelled by a dream concerning Darwin's experiments with the creation of artificial life.

On the surface level of a straightforward Gothic story *Frankenstein* is creepier than most and is also moving. Pathos becomes tragedy, and the central conflict is of strong interest. It is an obsessive, dramatic and symbolic hunt, like that of Coleridge's poem *The Ancient Mariner* (1797). The frenzy with which Frankenstein pursues the hidden knowledge, his disgust at the eight-foot tall monster he has made, his destruction of a half-finished wife for the monster, his remorse when the monster kills his brother, friend and wife, his chasing the monster in deepening despair—the reader is compulsively involved in this nightmarish experience.

The monster we can also identify with—we can recognise his misery at being repulsed in anger and hatred everywhere, and see how his crimes derive from bitter resentment of his creator.

The dramatic effect of this struggle is achieved by plain language, on the whole, which unobtrusively keeps the story on the move. There is some awkwardness—Frankenstein is inclined to 'gnash his teeth' too often, and where vivid detail is required, the narrative often lapses into abstractions. These are sometimes occasioned by the fact that Frankenstein keeps his dangerous discovery secret—which is somewhat irritating to the modern reader. As an example, in Frankenstein's ghastly researches in graveyards, charnel house and laboratory, where the author is expanding on a passage in Percy Shelley's poem *Alastor*, he has his eyes fixed on 'every object the most insupportable to the delicacy of the human feelings' and dabbles in 'the unhallowed damps of the grave', and so on.

Yet the description of the monster at the moment of coming alive is concrete enough.

His yellow skin scarcely covered the work of muscles and arteries beneath; his hair was of a lustrous black and flowing, his teeth of a pearly whiteness; but those luxuriances only formed a more horrid contrast with his watery eyes and straight black lips.

The description of typical romantic scenery in the Swiss mountains—sombre pine forests, mists wreathed around the peaks—is straightforward: it suffices to set the scene or establish the atmosphere, but does not slow down the momentum of the story.

The characterisation, apart from the two protagonists, is weak: they are moved around in the background like cardboard figures in a toy theatre, and all tend to speak in the same, stilted way. There are some improbabilities. The account of the monster being built of dead limbs does not convince, and many readers are incredulous at the way he lives undetected in a hovel from which he can see into a cottage, and is able to educate himself by eavesdropping when the family teach the language to an Arabian woman who visits them.

The structure of the narrative is also confusing: the story begins and ends in letters from the sea captain, Walton, who is likewise looking for the unknown in the Polar regions of the north, with Frankenstein's story enclosed in his, and the monster's inside Frankenstein's. To compound this defect, some of the episodes are too long-drawn-out.

What overrides these flaws and gives the central conflict depth and resonance is something not fully appreciated until the last pages, when the monster bends over the dead Frankenstein in grief and remorse, saying he will now burn himself on a funeral pyre, and we realise how much they have been part of one another. This theme has been hinted at several times, as for instance when Frankenstein said he considered the monster as his own spirit or vampire freed from the grave and impelled to kill those he loved. Their parallel lives, each hunting and being hunted by the other, suggest their interdependence as well as their hatred for one another.

The main message is thus dramatically and symbolically made clear: when reason is pushed to its limits, it breaks down, and the way in which the monster and his creator work towards each other's destruction implies that balance is the key to virtue, sanity and wholeness. The psychological pattern of Frankenstein's progressive disintegration together with the monster's growing evil are reflected in much later literature, notably in R. L. Stevenson's story of the respectable doctor who transformed himself, by a concoction of his discovery, into the evil obverse of his normal self, who led a parallel but disreputable life: *The Strange Case of Dr Jekyll and Mr Hyde* (1888).

Frankenstein expresses moral and political lessons as well as psychological truths, most clearly in the monster's reproaches to Frankenstein when he asks for a wife. Frankenstein is convinced at that point by the argument that his monster's vice derives from his misery, and that as his creator he is obliged to try to make him happy. This is developed as a political message in the description of the monster's experience of society as a whole, and these are echoes of Godwin's socialistic theories. As the monster tries to adapt to society, he soon discovers that property is divided, and that there is 'immense wealth and squalid poverty', that man hates and repulses the poor and the wretched, and that poverty and isolation breed bitterness and crime.

Frankenstein, or The Modern Prometheus is the novel's full title, and the author's husband based his poetic drama *Prometheus Unbound* on the legend of the demigod who stole fire from heaven for the benefit of mankind and was chained by Zeus to a rock as punishment. The reproaches made by the monster to his creator also echo those made by Milton's Satan in *Paradise Lost*. The creation of an artificial human being had earlier been treated in novels by Godwin and by Goethe.

Mary Shelley's book showed how the Gothic novel could widen its scope, and her kind of speculation on morality and man's scientific possibilities are also features of the best of today's science fiction. However, the power and vitality of *Frankenstein* derive partly from the fact that Mary Shelley did not quite understand what she was doing, and when she became more mature and had to understand what she wrote, her imagination lost its force. *Frankenstein*, the most enduring of the Gothic novels, is that very rare phenomenon: a classic that was originally a best seller and has remained extremely popular. Several films in the 1930's based on the novel, together with translations in numerous foreign languages, have made the name Frankenstein synonymous with horror in many parts of the world.

V. THE GOTHIC GENRE

Three other names are essential to the Gothic genre: Ann Radcliffe, Matthew Lewis and Charles Maturin.

The novels of Mrs Radcliffe have a sameness about them: they are not strong in characterization, nor in speculation. The story can build up towards a powerful climax, as it does throughout *The Italian* (1797), but in most of her other books the author dissipates the interest by over-complicating her plots.

Nevertheless, she is very gifted. In one word, she added poetry to the novel. This poetry is found in her descriptions of landscape, and in the moods and feelings of her characters, who are for the most part 'figures in a landscape'; they are in love with it, see divine order in it (as Wordsworth did), are manoeuvred by it (like some of Shakespeare's characters) and are dominated by it.

It is almost entirely a Mediterranean landscape which pervades her six novels, and is used as the setting for her repeated theme: she presents a beautiful heroine who undergoes many dangers, and is made mysterious by apparently supernatural happenings, before being able to marry the man she loves. This landscape, because she did not actually see it, Mrs Radcliffe took from the landscape painters Claude Lorraine, Nicolas Poussin, Salvator Rosa and others who satisfied 18th century writers' fascination with what was called the 'picturesque' (meaning at that time landscape that looked as if it had come out of a picture). She read the descriptions of travel journals and was influenced by the writing of Gray, Thomson and Rousseau.

Thus to Otranto's castle she added abbey ruins, often wreathed in mist, majestic mountains, sometimes 'frowning with forests of gloomy pine', and sunlit or rainswept glades, reflecting every mood. She uses weather as Hollywood much later learned to use it.

The Mysteries of Udolpho (1794) and *The Italian* are her best works. Apart from the settings, the novels present many of Walpole's Gothic elements—old manuscripts revealing secrets, and so on—but she keeps the supernatural at a distance. Emily, the heroine of *Udolpho*, faints at a terrible sight—a corpse's face being consumed by worms. She later discovers it was a picture—an image of wax used by penitents in the past for contemplation. Strange shadows and weird music turn out to have equally rational explanations. Radcliffe referred to her work as 'romance or phantasie', but the more concentrated later novel is less compromisingly Gothic.

Her wicked tyrants are her most interesting characters— Montoni in *Udolpho*, who marries Emily's aunt and tries to cheat her out of her inheritance, and the monk Schedoni in *The Italian* are lonely, strong-willed, handsome men with extraordinary passions, capable of great cruelty and also of great suffering. They show the strong influence of the bloodthirsty villains of the Elizabethan and Jacobean dramatists, while Walpole's Manfred (unconvincing though that character is) showed how some humanity could be added: on the other hand it was mainly Mrs Radcliffe's versions that inspired Maturin's, Byron's and Scott's romantic villains. She also improved on Walpole's talkative servants, giving them more depth and humour.

Udolpho is about sixteenth-century French people mainly and *The Italian* about seventeenth-century Italians, but in Gothic fashion they have the mentality and concerns of Mrs Radcliffe's contemporaries. In *The Italian* she made use of what had become another fascinating milieu for the Gothic writer—the Roman Catholic Church with the secretive, ritualistic life of convent and monastery, and the terrors of the Inquisition, whose officers imprisoned those suspected of heresy and exacted confessions from them by torture.

Unlike other Gothic writers she is moderate in her exploitation of all this. Most of the information for the background had to be derived at second hand, from such German authors as Schiller—she had read his *Ghost-Seer, or Appari-tionist* (1795)—and Marquis Grosse's *Genius*, which was translated as *Horrid Mysteries* in 1796. And she is typically vague, using the settings and rituals symbolically, rather than with any attempt at realism.

The author who first saw the huge potential in this subject-matter was Matthew Lewis. In *The Monk* (1796) Lewis used the scandalous accounts of goings-on in monasteries and in the prisons of the Inquisition to sensational and horrific effect. The exaggerations and implied condemnations were partly due to a desire to capitalize on a sudden resurgence of interest in such themes, because of the revival of the Spanish Inquisition in 1768; at the same time the development of different kinds of secret societies, mostly liberal and revolu-tionary, before and after the French Revolution of 1789 also played a part.

In fact, the period contains many historical personages whose experiences were as amazing as most of those of its fiction. There was Casanova, most famous of the world's lovers, and Mesmer, whose magnetism developed into hypnosis, and many more. Most Gothic was the self-styled Count Alessandro di Cagliostro (1743–95), 'the last and greatest of the sorcerers'. A physician, hypnotist, necro-mancer, alchemist, Rosicrucian, Grand Cophta of the Egyptian rite of Freemasonry, he was idolised by the high society of London and Paris, where he lived in great splendour and organised spectacular demonstrations of his talents. He was also imprisoned several times. His origins are obscure, but he was apparently born in Palermo, Sicily, as Giuseppe Balsamo. He is said to have been involved in the successful plot to steal a diamond necklace, when it was claimed that Queen Marie Antoinette wanted to buy it. He was tried by the Inquisition in Rome in 1790, and sentenced to life imprisonment.

Cagliostro's name has re-echoed in various literatures, in plays by Goethe and Catherine II, in a novel by George Sand and several by Alexandre Dumas, including the one trans-lated as *The Memoirs of a Physician*, where he is portrayed as chief of the Illuminati, who aimed to overthrow the thrones of Europe.

To return to Lewis's 'horrific effect', that term needs a little explanation, for there is an important distinction within the Gothic genre between terror and horror. Mrs Radcliffe's effects evoke terror, which implies 'uncertainty and obscurity', as she herself, having avoided Walpole's mistake of too much clarity, expressed it in an article: terror awakens the faculties whereas horror 'contracts, freezes and nearly annihilates them'. Horror includes repugnance as well as fear.

There had been horror in the last part of *Vathek* (1786) and there was to be horror in *Frankenstein* (1818) though not in a dominant mood, and the restraint of the latter owes much to Mrs Radcliffe. But Mary Shelley's father, William Godwin, wrote some Gothic novels, notably *Caleb Williams* (1794) and *St Leon* (1799), which have particular interest seen as halfway houses between terror and horror: these books place the emphasis on psychology, clearly presented, and eschew mystery.

St Leon has a Faustian theme, with a Schedoni-like character[1] ostracized by society conferring immortality on the hero. In *Caleb Williams* the eponymous hero discovers that two innocent people were hanged for a murder committed by a kind of superman figure called Falkland, and its use of crime in a novel format, with the story planned backwards—the technique developed so skilfully by Arthur Conan Doyle—was the beginning of the detective story.

These stories took the Gothic novel a stage further in its evolution, but no one was ready for the shock of *The Monk*, which had the effect of releasing passions and breaking mental barriers with the force of an earthquake. While he lacked the poetry or the subtlety of Mrs Radcliffe, whom he admired but found 'spineless', Lewis possessed the energy and instinct to make a credible marriage of reality with the supernatural—something which Walpole had failed and Mrs Radcliffe did not dare to do.

Ambrosio, the abbot of a Capuchin monastery in Madrid in about 1600, is a figure reminiscent of Macbeth. He is a devout man but also liable to strong passions and once he yields to temptation, he suffers a rapid decline into evil and despair. Unknowingly he rapes his sister and kills his mother.

[1] The villain of Mrs Radcliffe's *The Italian* (see p. 22).

In the prison of the Inquisition his hands are smashed to a pulp and nails torn; to escape the *auto da fe* (death by fire) he sells his soul to a winged devil, who nevertheless drops him over a cliff on to a jagged rock.

In a sub-plot, Agnes, the daughter of an aristocratic family who live in a haunted castle, is compelled to become a nun, and when discovered pregnant is condemned by the prioress to spend the rest of her life in a dark dungeon below the convent, surrounded by rotting corpses, toads and lizards, with 'cold vapours hovering in the air, the walls green with damp'. Agnes at one point is telling the story of her baby, which dies a few hours after birth:

I vowed not to part with it while I had life: its presence was my only comfort, and no persuasion could induce me to give it up. It soon became a mass of putridity, and to every eye was a loathsome and disgusting object—to every eye but a mother's. In vain did human feelings bid me recoil from this emblem of mortality with repugnance.... I endeavoured to retrace its features through the livid corruption with which they were overspread . . .

This is the most morbid passage in Lewis perhaps, but he carries it off with headlong readability—not such a common attribute of best sellers as may be imagined.

To the Gothic elements Lewis added unusual and 'real' ghosts (notably a Bleeding Nun who had been murdered in life, and made a bloodstained appearance in the castle every five years), whose restlessness is often ended when their bones are buried; the Wandering Jew of European mythology who insulted Christ and is compelled to wander the earth until Christ's Second Coming, and who in this version can stay no longer than fourteen days in the same place; wonderful demons; and sorcery.

Rich as Lewis's mixture was, the originality of his work, as with Walpole, resides in the recipe and the cooking rather than in the ingredients. His haunted castle comes from *Udolpho*, the evil monk Ambrosio derives from Montoni. (In turn, Ambrosio seems to have influenced Mrs Radcliffe's Schedoni, and the latter's Inquisition scenes—though very much in the background of her story—seem to derive from Lewis). The gore and the eroticism of Lewis and the obsessive scenes of death in the vaults come from Elizabethan and Jacobean dramatists. Lewis was also well read in German literature, had studied Part 1 of Goethe's *Faust*, and Schiller. The Bleeding Nun Story and Ambrosio's way of death were borrowed from German tales of terror.

Otranto influenced the *Sturm und Drang* (Storm and Stress) movement of the 1770s, and later numerous translations or adaptations were made in England at the turn of the century of German novels, notably Bürger's *Leonore* (1796) and translations of Goethe and Schiller. There were three main kinds of German novel—chivalric, novels about robbers, and horror novels—and they added bandits, monks, poisonings and tortures to the English Gothic elements.

The borrowings of course went back and forth. The German Hoffmann, for example, learned from Lewis and in turn influenced Maturin and Emily Brontë's *Wuthering Heights*. Lewis's work had numerous imitators, Percy Shelley's rather weak novels being among them, and later some very good writers on the supernatural—Edgar Allan Poe and Sheridan Le Fanu. French works enriched this traffic. The translation of Richardson into French generated numerous French heroines of sensibility, who were then imitated by British writers, together with Prévost's horror elements.

Charles Maturin's *Melmoth the Wanderer* (1820) is as astonishing and, in its own way, as fruitful a work as *The Monk*. It is an amalgam of terror and horror: it displays an awkwardness and pretentiousness that at times make it exasperating reading, but it nevertheless contains in the eponymous hero/villain one of the most memorable of all Gothic diabolic characters. The necromantic Melmoth has bought with his soul 150 years of youth from the Devil, and in his wanderings through the seventeenth and eighteenth centuries attempts to find new victims: people undergoing extreme suffering are offered the chance of exchanging places with Melmoth, if they give up their souls. They all refuse. This makes a unifying theme for a collection of different stories, although Maturin scarcely exploits its dramatic possibilities to the full. The subjects include the Englishman Stanton, who is losing his sanity in a London asylum, and Isadora, whom Melmoth marries in Madrid. They are married by the hand of a dead hermit, and the witness is the ghost of a murdered domestic servant. Isadora suffers at the hands of the Inquisition. Her child by Melmoth dies in prison, and she dies of a broken heart after refusing Melmoth's offer.

More suggestive and less salacious than Lewis as he creates his worlds of torment, Maturin crammed into a very long novel most of the Gothic properties—there are a fair number of parricides and maniacs, monks whipping the flesh off a novice as he flees, Jews in cellars surrounded by the skeletons of their families—and learned from Lewis how to use the supernatural. But these elements are subsidiary to the terrors that go on *inside* people's minds. This is his original contribution to the Gothic novel: his analysis of the disintegration of the mind under extreme suffering and harassment.

An attempt is made to force the illegitimate son of the Duke of Moncada into a vocation by his family and by monks that astonishingly incorporates many of the mind-bending techniques we have associated with the world-wars of this century. These episodes and the other Goyaesque prison, monastery and asylum scenes stand out vividly in this rambling work: it suffers, however, from a surfeit of scholarly jokes and from the confusing Chinese-box structure of story within story which has been noted in *Frankenstein*, and was common in 18th and early 19th century novels.

Maturin was an inspiration not only for writers with Gothic associations such as Poe, but also, directly or indirectly, for many different kinds of writers—for writers of suspense stories in Britain such as Wilkie Collins and R. L. Stevenson, for psychological terror stories such as Henry James's *The Turn of the Screw*, for Oscar Wilde (especially *The Picture of Dorian Gray*) and for the modern detective novel. The great Italian classic of Manzoni, *I Promessi Sposi* (*The Betrothed*) (1825), has a long section in which a young woman is forced to take the monastic vows. The most extensive influence of *Melmoth* was on French literature— on Victor Hugo, Dumas père, and Balzac (who wrote a sequel, *Melmoth Reconciled* in translation) among many others.

A disappointing ending—Melmoth released from his wandering, suddenly ages and jumps off a cliff, leaving his handkerchief behind—does not detract from the powerful impression which the character leaves on the mind. His mysteriousness is enhanced by lack of detail about his appearance, except for references to his hypnotic eyes, lighted with "preternatural lustre', to his weird, desperate laugh, or the furrows of agony which cross his face. The power he exerts over the imagination lies in the tremendous contradictions of his being: the force of his personality is such that he appals and fascinates all who meet him—yet he fails to tempt any prospective victim. He scorns the weakness of some of the Church's servants, yet is impelled by satanic envy and destructiveness. He accepts his chosen fate, and yet is continually tormented by a glimmer of hope.

Melmoth, like Lewis's monk, as well as inspiring greater writers, was of course vulgarized in many imitations. To add to the other 'damned immortal' associations there is in him a strong suggestion of the mythical vampire, the 'undead' who return to life each night and suck the blood of people, who then also become vampires. The most talented of the writers on vampires, such as Bram Stoker (1847-1912), whose best novel was *Dracula* (1897), put much of Melmoth into their protagonists, though there was also the example of the already-mentioned *The Vampyre* by Polidori, published a year before *Melmoth*.

The work of E. T. A. Hoffmann (1776-1822), one of the finest writers of horror tales that Germany has produced, was among the German influences on Maturin, particularly in the black magic business. Hoffmann wrote one definitely Gothic novel, translated as *The Devil's Elixir* in 1824, about a monk succumbing to the Devil's temptations. He had the same interest as Maturin in powerful minds, whether strangely hypnotic or in league with the Devil, and this concern is much in evidence in the three *Tales of Hoffmann* that formed the basis of Offenbach's opera. In *The Sandman* a young student, under the spell of an evil magician Coppelius, falls in love with a doll, and finally jumps off a high building to his death. In another, a young man loses his reflection to his lover, and in the third a consumptive girl singer prefers singing herself to death to living safely and obediently.

Hoffmann can be over-morbid and lacks the psychological insights of Maturin, but for a hothouse originality that infected Dostoyevsky among others he deserves a mention here among the best practitioners of the Gothic genre, before we trace the various ramifications of the Gothic spirit in later literature.

VI. GOTHIC AND POPULAR

The influence on English literature of the German terror-romance at the turn of the eighteenth century is illustrated by Jane Austen's satire upon the Gothic novel, *Northanger Abbey*, in which she shows how such literature could reduce its readers' capacity for enlightenment. Completed in 1803, the publishers held it back till 1818, apparently afraid that it would do harm to the Gothic market. In the city of Bath Isabella Thorpe is recommended to read seven 'horrid' novels, and these have been analysed in Michael Sadleir's essay, *The Northanger Novels*. Only one, *Clermont*, a rhapso-dical romance dated between 1793 and 1798, is not German in provenance or inspiration. *The Castle of Wolfenbach*, *Orphan of the Rhine*, *The Mysterious Warning*, and *Midnight Bell* are substantially Gothic and heavily German-influenced, the first strongly suggesting *Otranto*, the third *Udolpho*. Then there are *Necromancer of the Black Forest*, with content directly borrowed from the German, and pointing to *Melmoth*, and *Horrid Mysteries*, already mentioned, a translation from German.

The wholehearted Gothic novel, however, lost favour and quality after 1820. It had fallen into the hands of unskilled, imitative writers: the result was that either the repetition of horrors in vulgar copies of Lewis blunted appetites, or the dependence on Radcliffe-type explanations became tedious. The decline of the Gothic was assisted by different kinds of novel—notably Eaton Standard Barrett's *The Heroine: or The Adventures of Cherubina* (1813), Scott's *Waverley* and Jane Austen's *Northanger Abbey* of 1818. Both the first and last of these satirized the genre, but it was a very slow process

(Jane Austen received £10 for *Northanger Abbey*, while over twenty years earlier Mrs Radcliffe had received £500 and £800 for *Udolpho* and *The Italian* respectively). From about 1830 a lurid kind of Gothic continued in series of magazine stories such as 'Terrific Tales', or longer 'shockers', with screaming covers.

As Gothic literature declined, popular literature of other kinds, but much of it having Gothic attributes, boomed. For with the newly invented paper-making machines and rotary presses of the early nineteenth century, literature for the masses was now being produced in quantity. Some of the appetite for the strange had been and was being deflected from Gothic to Romantic—to Shelley, Byron and Southey, whose *Thalaba the Destroyer* (1801) used Oriental mythology and encouraged reprinting of *The Arabian Nights*. In spite of the Northanger list, the borrowings from German of popular literature as a whole were mainly romances, often without the supernatural, such as Bürger's *Leonore*, translated as *The Chase* in 1796 by Scott, and folk tales such as those collected by the Grimm Brothers. What is of interest for the moment is that some of the new kinds of popular literature exploited Gothic elements and qualities in various ways.

The supernatural, for instance, was often used as a divine agency to support the accepted morality that frequently provided the message. A typical plot, for example, shows the evil monk being thwarted in his designs on the maiden he has imprisoned when part of the monastery collapses on top of him, while the maiden makes her escape.

The influence of the German tales of terror spread beyond Gothic novels to many other kinds of popular literature. *The Monk* and *Melmoth* owe an obvious debt to the Faust legend: this was also combined very effectively, from the late thirties, with the German werewolf theme—in G. W. M. Reynold's *Wagner the Werewolf* (1847) a German peasant is given perpetual youth by Satan provided he becomes a werewolf every seven years. Imitations of German stories often had German characters.

There were many satires of the Gothic novel, and the over-sensitive heroine of both the Gothic romance and the sentimental romance that preceded it was a frequent butt.

31

Barrett's *The Heroine* (1813) provides at times a hilarious send-up of the excesses of Mrs Radcliffe and Lewis, using phrases from the originals to make the parodies stick. Cherubina, a country girl who suffers various 'Gothic' adventures looking for her lost parents says: 'Oft times I sit and weep, I know not why; and then I weep to find myself weeping. Then, when I can weep, I weep at having nothing to weep at . . .'

Jane Austen borrowed much of the situation of *Udolpho's* Volume IV, chapter 4 for chapter 20 of *Northanger Abbey*. The heroine, Catherine Morland, is shown through the old abbey to her room, where someone had died twenty years before, by the old housekeeper, Dorothy. Catherine's head is full of Gothic novels, and she expects at least a secret passage, and perhaps an imprisoned wife somewhere and a few skeletons. But all she finds, in a japanned cabinet, is what appears to be an old manuscript, which turns out, in the morning, to be a laundry list.

Jane Austen has a lot of fun with the Gothic conventions, and although the satire is gentle and subtle enough in the novel, her dislike of the unnaturalness of so much Gothic heroics is very clear, and the message, in this earliest published work—that the use of imagination without reason can dangerously damage one's judgement—was to be developed in her later novels. Like Catherine, the heroines of *Pride and Prejudice, Sense and Sensibility* and the others would suffer in the real world, and lose their illusions.

Thomas Love Peacock, a friend of Shelley, satirised in *Nightmare Abbey* (1818) the way in which the poet and his followers derived their schemes for changing the world, not only from Shelley's father-in-law from that year, Godwin, but from Gothic romances and German tragedies and tales of terror—the way they made use, for example, of such secret societies as the Illuminati, founded by the German Weishaupt in 1776, who considered that they possessed special enlightenment, believed in republicanism and were organized like freemasons. Shelley is represented by Scythrop Glowry in the book and Mary Shelley as Stella, but it is a problem for today's reader that many of the characters cannot be traced to the originals who suggested them, and

'The Sleep of Reason Produces Monsters'. Etching from *Los Caprichos* by
FRANCISCO GOYA *by courtesy of the Witt Collection, The Courtauld Institute of Art*

Ruins of the Baths at Hadrian's Villa. Etching from *Vedute di Roma* by G. B. PIRANESI (see pp 8 and 10) *by courtesy of the British Architectural Library, RIBA*

Prison with central staircase flanked by grilled windows. Etching from *Carceri d'Invenzione* by G. B. PIRANESI (see pp 8 and 10). 'Anxiety with no possibility of escape is the main theme of the Gothic tales' (Mario Praz) *by courtesy of the British Architectural Library, RIBA*

'The Nightmare' by HENRY FUSELI *by courtesy of the Goethe Museum, Frankfurt*

since Peacock is very close to the events he was living through, the obscurities are many.

For the student of Gothic literature, nevertheless, the satirical wit of *Nightmare Abbey* provides plenty of compensation. There is a scene between Scythrop and Marionetta (based on Shelley's first wife Harriet Westbrook), in which he suggests that they drink their mixed blood as a sacrament of love—(they would see 'visions of transcendental illumination and soar on the wings of ideas into the space of pure intelligence')—that echoes a scene in *Horrid Mysteries* between Rosalia and Don Carlos. However, Marionetta 'had not so strong a stomach as Rosalia, and turned sick at the proposition'. Peacock's aim in *Nightmare Abbey*, as he expressed it in a letter to Shelley, was to 'bring to a sort of philosophical focus a few of the morbidities' of the literature of the time. It is light-hearted burlesque and is diffused over the wide target of both Gothic and Romantic extravagances.

VII. GOTHIC AND ROMANTIC

The imaginations of the pre-Romantic poets, notably Blair, Blake, Burns, Collins and Young, were strongly drawn to nocturnal themes, to graveyards haunted by ghosts and demons, and to the imagery of dreams and nightmares. They were stimulated by the treatment of such themes and imagery to be found here and there in Percy's *Reliques of Ancient English Poetry* of 1765, and James Macpherson's *The Poems of Ossian* (1760–63), in the *Arabian Nights*, and in cheaply printed collections of medieval legends such as those concerning Dr Faustus and the Wandering Jew. And even earlier than this we find such a representative poem as Collins's *Ode to Fear* (1751)

> Thou to whom the World unknown
> With all its shadowy shapes is shown.
> Who see'st, appall'd, the unreal scene
> While Fancy lifts the veil between
>   Ah, Fear! Ah, frantic Fear
>   I see, I see thee near.

The Romantic movement in poetry and the Gothic movement in the novel shared some of their origins—their interest in medievalism and in the supernatural, for instance. At times, Gothic qualities appear to be one aspect of Romanticism. Writers moved from one to the other. Mrs Radcliffe, Lewis and Maturin inserted verses into their novels; Lewis's ballads influenced the poetry of Scott, Shelley, Byron and Coleridge, while the poets experimented with the Gothic novel and drama.

The Gothic principles expounded by Walpole in his preface to the second edition of *Otranto*—to create extraordinary, or supernatural, situations, but people them with believable characters behaving believably—has a strong affinity with Coleridge's recipe for Romanticism, expressed thirty years later in the preface to the *Lyrical Ballads*. The interest in libertarian ideas, in spiritual worlds, in the grotesque and the horrible in both Gothic and Romantic has been sufficiently noted.

Where Romanticism and Gothicism part company most conspicuously, perhaps, is in the former's insistence that Beauty is most closely associated with pain, desire, sorrow. The Gothic novelists were well aware of the hypnotic appeal of their satanic villains, with their 'virile beauty' (which Baudelaire attributed to the perfect type of Milton's Satan) and which they flaunted as extravagantly as their suffering and cruelty; but whereas the novelists exploited the characters for dramatic and horrific effects, the Romantic poets philosophised about the phenomenon.

'Our sweetest songs are those that tell of saddest thought', Shelley says in *To a Skylark*, and Keats says that melancholy 'dwells with Beauty—Beauty that must die'. There are poems about the beauty of the Medusa—one of the three Gorgons of Greek myth, with snakes for hair, whose glance turned the beholder to stone. One by Shelley contains the line "Tis the tempestuous loveliness of terror'. Baudelaire expressed his own and other spirits' attraction to the ugly and deformed as '*la soif de l'inconnu et le goût de l'horrible*' (the thirst for the unknown, the taste for the horrible).

The Gothic descriptions of corpses and skeletons, mingling fascination and loathing, are refined in the Romantic poets to a longing for what is beyond death, in a spiritual, or un-known, world—for what cannot be described. Keats expressed this idealism most memorably in lines of *Ode on a Grecian Urn*:

> Heard melodies are sweet, but those unheard
> Are sweeter . . .

Death to the Romantics is a release from ugliness. On the death of Keats, Shelley rejoices that age would not spoil that beautiful spirit. The idea is extended by Romantic extremists/outsiders such as Baudelaire, who searched for beauty where death and despair were near—in the hospitals for the poor and the brothels of Paris. Imagination was all; it was the feelings that were to be stimulated rather than the mind.

The erotic sensibility underlying the Romantic attitude is the subject of Mario Praz's classic study *The Romantic Agony*, and there is space here only to mention the chief aim of the book, though it has suggested many of my comments in this chapter. Praz pursues the relations between beauty and pain, sexual desire and cruelty as one pattern in the carpet of Romanticism. For his thesis he ransacked British, French and Italian literatures, and naturally gave plenty of attention to the Marquis de Sade (without overstating his few literary merits), the Decadents and various forms of algolagnia, including flagellation.

The term Romantic has been obscured and devalued by its loose application to literature of all ages that emphasises imagination and the subjective at the expense of the rational and ordered, which follows rules. But even in the stricter, late eighteenth-century and early nineteenth-century sense, and confining the term to those writers who were consciously following a definite, Romantic aim, the movement has a much less exact connotation of historical period than the Gothic. Romanticism is a current that can be traced right through to today, while Gothicism is a stream that goes underground, out of sight, for long periods, and then reappears in different forms. Part of the reason for the decline in Gothic as a genre was the absorption of many of its aspects by Romanticism.

Byron acknowledged that

> Otway, Radcliffe, Schiller, Shakespeare's art,
> Had stamped her image in me.

The Byronic, or Romantic, hero—the Fatal Man of the Romantics—in the form of the Giaour, the Corsair, Childe Harold, Lara, and Manfred—all pale, beautiful, haunted by guilt, with amazing eyes, melancholy, superior and proud, mostly also misanthropic, ruthless, mysterious, heroic and villainous—clearly derives from the writers he singles out. Most directly they come from Mrs Radcliffe's Montoni and Schedoni. The influence of Schiller's adventurous, suffering, robbers came both directly and from Lewis's *The Monk* via Schedoni, and Milton's Satan is a shadow over all. Setting Mrs Radcliffe's Schedoni—

His cowl, too, as it threw a shade over the livid paleness of his face, increased its severe character, and gave an effect to his large melancholy eye, which approached to horror . . . his physiognomy . . . bore the traces of many passions, which seemed to have fixed the features they no longer animated . . . his eyes were so piercing that they seemed to penetrate, at a single glance, into the hearts of men, and to read their most secret thoughts; few persons could support their scrutiny, or even endure to meet them twice. . . .'

beside Byron's Giaour—

> Dark and unearthly is the scowl
> That glares beneath his dusky cowl.
> The flash of that dilating eye
> Reveals too much of time gone by;
> Though varying, indistinct its hue,
> Oft will his glance the gazer rue,
> For in it lurks that nameless spell,
> Which speaks, itself unspeakable,
> A spirit yet unquell'd and high
> That claims and keeps ascendancy. . . .

—the correspondences are clear.

As well as drawing together all these sources, Byron added much of himself, a man who lived, loved and drank so hard that at his death at thirty-six his brain and heart showed the signs of very advanced age.

Byron's Manfred, talking of Astarte, provided the motto for the 'fatal men' of Romantic literature: 'I loved her, and destroy'd her'. Vampires are these fatal men in their most symbolic form. Byron mentions vampires in *The Giaour*, and, as mentioned, gave Polidori the sketch that became the first vampire novel in English. Vampires were invariably men in the first half of the eighteenth century; thereafter, they are mainly represented as women. Most vampire novels vulgarised Gothic themes.

The Wandering Jew, which became such a significant Gothic motif, has an unforgettable characterization in Coleridge's guilt-tortured *Ancient Mariner* (and later turns up in Keats's *Endymion* and Shelley's *Alastor*). Piranesi's etchings haunted Coleridge as well as Walpole and Beckford. In *Confessions of an Opium-Eater* Thomas De Quincey tells how Coleridge described to him Piranesi's etching entitled *Dreams*: staircases, one after the other, with Piranesi standing at the top of each one, before an abyss.

There is a close association between dreams—and their importance for the creative writer—and drugs. De Quincey in his *Confessions* held that dreams crystallized the particles of past experience into a symbolic pattern. In an opium-induced dream the writer could see how the crystallization took place. The influence of opium can be seen in Poe, Baudelaire, Crabbe, Coleridge, Wilkie Collins and Francis Thompson who regularly took it, and De Quincey's thesis has much corroboration in the evidence from these writers that they learned from opium, by observing their imaginations at work.

However, in her study of the subject, *Opium and the Romantic Imagination*, Alethea Hayter finds no clear pattern of influence on the works. Having acknowledged the benefits mentioned, she finds that the overall long-term effect is harmful because the drug 'detaches the writer from sympathy with what is observed', and because it works against coherence and damages 'the power to detect damage'.

She concludes her book brilliantly, by imagining a writer's thoughts inside a typical Piranesi prison, as a way of representing the effects of opium.

Both interior and exterior settings in the Romantic poets often produce unmistakable echoes of the Gothic novels they consumed. Coleridge's ballad *Christabel* is a masterpiece of Gothic, with its haunted castle, and moonlight gleaming through torn clouds. Wordsworth in his verse play *The Borderers*, as well as borrowing a good deal of its content from Schiller's *The Robbers* and from various Gothic fictions, has learned from Mrs Radcliffe how to put terror into the shapes and moods of natural scenery. Byron's drama, *Manfred*, has Gothic halls, a tower with a secret room, and demons, and his *Childe Harold* has picturesque passages that could have been written by Mrs Radcliffe, as could many of those in Keats and Shelley. Keats in *The Eve of St Agnes* plundered *Udolpho* for the castle, shadowy passages, moonlight and feudal jollifications. When he attempts gorgeous descriptions, as in *Lamia*, it is Beckford that comes to mind. Shelley, apart from his two Gothic novels *Zastrozzi* (1810) and *St Irvine* (1811), has bits of Gothic everywhere. The *Cenci*, in the words of Varma, has 'the ferocity of algolagnic sensibility'.

In early nineteenth-century prose fiction, the Gothic spirit, unmistakable as it is, manifests itself in different ways. Scott, the admirer of Mrs Radcliffe, took Gothic details to fill in his pictures and was rarely unfaithful to history. The Gothic manifestations of the Brontës are very interesting. Charlotte's Rochester in *Jane Eyre* and Emily's Heathcliff in *Wuthering Heights* have strong resemblances to Schedoni and Byron's Manfred: Rochester's locked-up mad wife is reminiscent of one in Mrs Radcliffe's *A Sicilian Romance*, and *Wuthering Heights* has nightmares and ghosts. Both novels have Gothic weather, and when Emily falters, she has Heathcliff 'crushing his nails into his palms, and grinding his teeth to subdue the maxillary convulsions'. But the stories, with all their passions, are rooted in the reality of the simple, domestic life of the English countryside: their emotive power is enhanced by their credibility.

It is appropriate to end this chapter with a Romantic-

Gothic writer of great ability and seminal importance. With no author, perhaps, is the influences game easier to play than with the American Edgar Allan Poe (1809-49). His heroes have affinities with the lonely outsiders of the American literary tradition in Melville and Hawthorne, but more obviously and strikingly he learned a great deal from Coleridge, Byron, Keats, Shelley and De Quincey. The main impulse for his tales of horror was the German Gothic literature.

Poe's reputation is much higher in France than in Britain or the United States; he is regarded as the leading spirit of Symbolism, whom Baudelaire, Mallarmé, Verlaine and Rimbaud followed with reverence. Even more, if Jules Verne is the father of modern science fiction, Poe is the grandfather, and he also significantly developed the detective story, with lessons for Stevenson and Arthur Conan Doyle. 'The Murders in the Rue Morgue' (1841) was based on an actual American case, transposed to Paris. Poe's powers of deduction were such that he could work out the ending of a Dickens novel by reading the first chapter.

'The Rue Morgue' is as much a story of horror as of detection. It is the horror tale that is Poe's *forte*—his only attempt at a novel was unfinished. At the beginning, under the influence of German tales, he had all the familiar Gothic machinery, but very speedily developed his own, highly individual style. He then rejected the label of 'Germanic', with its associations of extravagant gloom and 'pseudo-horror', and wrote: 'I maintain that terror is not of Germany but of the soul—that I have deduced this terror only from its legitimate sources, and only to its legitimate results'.

Poe added psychology: his main interest, more so than Maturin's, was in what went on *inside* his protagonists' minds, and his descriptions of doom-laden settings and furniture are genuinely, and symbolically, relevant to the tale, not just spurious additions. The study is generally profound because most of the protagonists, like Usher in 'The Fall of the House of Usher' ('there were but peculiar sounds, and these from stringed instruments, which did not inspire him with horror') are endowed and cursed with an abnormally cultivated sensitivity. Estranged from reality, often inhabiting heavily curtained rooms, they lose their sanity and sometimes their lives. They are driven back into the prison of themselves. That is a horror symbolized in other tales by being drowned in whirlpools (as in 'A Descent into the Maelstrom'), being buried alive (as in 'The Cask of Amontillado'), being subjected to the most ingenious tortures the Spanish Inquisition could devise (as in 'The Pit and the Pendulum'). After Poe the Gothic spirit became diffused. The Romantic movement had particularly exploited its supernatural aspects, and many different kinds of novel and tale would do the same.

VIII. MODERN GOTHIC

From the 1830s to today there has been a flood of literature descended from the Gothic. Most directly, there have been fiction about the supernatural, including stories of ghosts, vampires, werewolves and other weird transformations; detective and thriller fiction; fantasy and science fiction. Some of this is mediocre, escapist stuff, but there are more great names to put beside those already mentioned, and many other writers of exceptional interest.

The better writers on the supernatural achieve their effects with the minimum of props, and it is the interior, psychological effects that are significant. They learned from the great nineteenth-century novelists and some of the master story-tellers how to do it. Balzac's *Melmoth Reconcilié* has been mentioned. In *The Wild Ass's Skin (Le Peau de Chagrin*, 1831) he uses a magic device. The hero, Raphael, shares many of the characteristics of Faust as well as of the author himself. The plot pivots round a magic piece of leather found in an antique shop, which grants its owner's wishes, but shrinks each time the spell is invoked, ironically shortening his life.

Another French writer, Alexandre Dumas, apart from his long list of historical novels, dealt with the supernatural. *The Wolf Leader* (1857) uses that popular combination of Wandering Jew and werewolf themes, becoming a werewolf for periods being the Devil's condition for continuing life, and Dumas also wrote a number of vampire tales. The American

Nathaniel Hawthorne, in both tales and novels, makes considerable use of the supernatural, or the weird, to symbolize evil. *The House of the Seven Gables* (1851) involves a family curse—the ghosts of ancestors haunting a house because one of the family condemned an innocent man—and this is a theme which Hawthorne handled in several works.

'The Queen of Spades' (1834), a short story by the greatest of Russian poets, Pushkin, uses the supernatural in a simple but masterly way, which combines irony and fantasy, and requires no aid from white sheets and clanking chains. It has reverberated in other literatures, was the basis of Tchaikovsky's opera and the ballet *The Three Card Trick*. Hermann, an army officer, is an austere, self-absorbed, obsessed 'hero' cast in a fatal, Romantic mould; he won Dostoyevsky's acclaim and may have suggested the latter's Raskolnikov in *Crime and Punishment*. Hermann threatens an old Countess with a pistol in order to get from her a card trick that will win him a fortune gambling, and she dies of shock. The pistol was unloaded. Her ghost reveals the card trick to him, but he is foiled by her at the last round of the card game, when instead of the Ace expected, the Queen of Spades appears. It is her features which appear on the card: she winks, and he goes mad.

The Russian Gogol in his short stories develops a Hoffmann-like fantasy. Such stories as 'The Nose', in which that appendage, having been shaved off, takes on a life of its own and drives a carriage round St Petersburg, is whimsy rather than witty, but there are few doubts about 'The Portrait' (1835)—which continues living to express the evil of a wicked merchant—and 'The Overcoat' (1842), one of the most famous of all ghost stories.

Charles Dickens wrote many supernatural tales within the novels and for the magazines he edited between 1850 and 1870, encouraging contemporaries, notably Wilkie Collins and Bulwer Lytton to produce them. Henry James's *The Turn of the Screw* (1898) is about two children possessed by the evil spirits of dead servants. Franz Kafka, whose blend of allegory, fantasy and horror, defying easy categorization, has been a strong influence on so much modern fiction since, wrote three works that demand mention: *The Castle* (1930),

The Trial (1937), and the long-short story *Metamorphosis* (1937), in which a young man becomes a cockroach. Like Poe and Kafka, Guy de Maupassant put many of his own phobias and nightmares into his tales of supernatural terror before he died in 1893, at 42, syphilitic and insane.

The Irishman Sheridan Le Fanu (1814–73) was, like Poe, a link between the Gothic and the psychological horror of modern times. In novels and numerous tales he dealt with all aspects of the supernatural, and his mastery of suspense and ability to sustain an atmosphere without slipping into bathos or unconscious humour (a tightrope for the best writers in the genre) have given him the status of a classic—though a neglected one. His tales show his strength, rather than his novels. Among his masterpieces are the short stories 'Carmilla', about a Countess vampire, which achieves psychological insight into lesbianism without detracting from or vulgarizing the horrific effect, and 'Green Tea', about a man haunted by a strange creature resembling a monkey.

Of the long list of British writers in this genre during the Victorian period, Lord Bulwer-Lytton, with the superb story 'The Haunted and the Haunters' (1859) among historical and occult works; Lord Dunsany (1878–1957) with his fantasies of other worlds, many containing a chilling evil presence at the heart of them; M. R. James (1862–1936), an ingenious but much less frightening version of Sheridan Le Fanu, his inspirer; and Walter de la Mare, the poet, who wrote various collections of ghost stories, and whose novels include *Memoirs of a Midget* (1921), about a woman two feet tall—all these are well worth reading.

Opinions vary on H. P. Lovecraft. His works, though readable, lack literary merit, and elements of racism and snobbery alienate many readers. But his fantasy worlds and weird tales are original, and enthusiasts for Gothic will admire his formidable knowledge of the literature of the supernatural. His critical work, *Supernatural Horror in Literature* was published in 1927. More recent supernatural stories have shown an interest in magic, witchcraft and the occult in general.

A pattern for the development of the detective novel can

be made out as follows: Godwin, Lewis, Poe (the key figure), Wilkie Collins, Sheridan Le Fanu. Le Fanu's *The House by the Churchyard* (1863) is a fine example. Collins wrote two compelling detective novels—*The Woman in White* (1860) and *The Moonstone* (1868), well written, well worked out, and sustaining the 'mysteries' (as much detective fiction used to be called) throughout. *The Woman in White* is one of the forerunners and best examples of what are called 'thrillers': added to the suspense/detection interest, there are adventures and more recognizable (though controlled) Gothic elements in this work, including a persecuted heroine and a devilish (though believable) criminal. *The Moonstone* is one of the best of detective novels.

These labels are only rough guides, particularly as detective fiction is so voluminous. Both detective novels and thrillers use such Gothic techniques as ingenious murder methods, the theft of wills and other documents, wrongful suspicion, suspense, mysteries explained at the end. City streets replace castle corridors. The persecuted heroine is still there, if dryer-eyed and more able to look after herself. The Gothic hero-villain may have become a mad scientist, a much nastier Frankenstein, as in Ian Fleming's thrillers, or he may be the detective, with an intellect far superior to that of anyone around him, and the evil refined down to mere eccentricity. Perhaps the most famous detective in fiction is Arthur Conan Doyle's egotistic Sherlock Holmes, a pale thin man, of astonishing deductive ability (like Poe's), who takes opium and plays the violin. He was the progenitor of a long line of detectives, including Dorothy L. Sayers's Lord Peter Wimsey, Agatha Christie's Hercule Poirot and the Belgian writer Simenon's Maigret.

The three English writers were generally concerned with plot rather than sensation, but they did write books that contained horror. One of Doyle's best novels, in fact, is *The Hound of the Baskervilles* (1901), a Sherlock Holmes story where the detective is confronted not by a werewolf but a vicious hound with a villainous master. Sayers put together large anthologies entitled *Great Short Stories of Detection, Mystery and Horror* (1929–34), and Agatha Christie also had a penchant for the weird, which surfaced in parts of many novels and in a fine volume of tales entitled *The Hound of Death* (1933).

Iris Murdoch, a philosopher as well as a novelist, uses Gothic elements in some of her novels, notably in *The Unicorn* and *The Time of the Angels*, the first set in a remote, coastal region, with a castle, a swamp and cliffs above the sea. She gives the landscape a romantic power over the characters, and the castle is a prison for the chief character, Hannah Crean-Smith, cursed by her husband to remain inside for seven years. The Gothic setting and situation enable the author to fabricate a mythical environment in which she can explore various ideas about good and evil, guilt and innocence, and freedom. *The Time of the Angels* is set in a rectory.

The earlier mention of 'mad scientists' suggests the link between the Gothic novel and science fiction. On the model of *Frankenstein* the best science fiction has some concern for science's role in the future and often has political and moral messages to deliver.

The works of Jules Verne, much of H. G. Wells, Aldous Huxley's *Brave New World* and George Orwell's *1984* are among the most original kinds, but in the past thirty or forty years, alongside an avalanche of SF pulp fiction, there has been a great variety of fascinating and vital literature in this sphere, on both sides of the Atlantic, the 'fantasy' and 'pure SF' labels becoming increasingly difficult to keep distinct. The work of the American Ray Bradbury (born 1920), mainly in short story form, is better described as fantasy. Kurt Vonnegut and Isaac Azimov, also American, are good as well as prolific.

Among the SF novels of Brian Aldiss is an ingenious commentary on Mary Shelley's novel called *Frankenstein Un-bound* (1973), in which Joe Bodenland, owing to a space/time rupture, is transported back from the United States of the twenty-first century to the Switzerland of 1816. Here he meets Mary Shelley, the poet Shelley, whose wife she is about to become, Byron, and the characters of the novel *Frankenstein* that is being worked on. J. G. Ballard has concerned himself with what he calls 'inner space' (rather than outer). Many of his novels and stories deal with the effects on the mind of the environment and of natural disasters. Colin Wilson (born 1931) has written a combination of horror and SF in *Space Vampires* (1976). Michael Moorcock (born 1939) is an extremely prolific writer who exploits various techniques in fantasy, SF and traditional genres and is building a sizeable reputation. Angela Carter's writings have been called, in some desperation, 'Gothic science fiction'. Mostly her works are an unusual blend of the two.

IX. IN OTHER MEDIA

Angela Carter wrote a fantasia of the Dracula story for radio recently, called *Vampirella*. 'My daughter, the last of the line' Dracula says in this, 'through whom I now project a modest, posthumous existence, believes . . . that she may be made whole by human feeling'. There has been much work in the Gothic lineage done for radio, both adaptations and original work. What can misfire or become unconsciously absurd on the page or when represented on film or TV screen may take compelling and frightening shape in the mind encouraged to imagine. As the child said, when asked why he preferred radio to television, 'the pictures are better'.

Where the effect has to be intimate, where the terror can be projected in subtle ways, where images can be unsensationally charged with symbolism, and where the atmosphere can be built up slowly and surely, then television can be a very effective medium. Ghost stories in a mainly domestic setting have tended to work best, there have been satisfying TV versions of such works as *Dracula* to confound these generalizations.

The attraction of Gothic horror for the cinema is obvious. One of the most influential films ever made is the classic German horror film, Robert Wiene's *The Cabinet of Dr. Caligari* (1920). The identity of Caligari, an eighteenth century Italian showman who hypnotised a somnambulist and used him to commit murders, is taken over by the crazed director of a psychiatric institute. The script by Carl Mayer and Haas Janowitz has the flavour of Hoffmann. Mary Shelley's novel had been filmed in 1908, 1916 and

45

1920, but these versions no longer exist, and Hollywood's *Frankenstein* of 1931 remains the classic, with Boris Karloff as the monster. This was followed by sequels adding to the story—*Bride of Frankenstein* (1935) whose ambiguous title compounded people's inclination to make the name refer to the monster instead of the scientist, and *Son of Frankenstein* (1939), and there have been many imitations since. 'As a man I should destroy him, as a scientist I should bring him back to life', the scientist says in *Son of Frankenstein*. The effect of the films is to make fears and suspicions about the powers of the scientist explicit, by the vivid imagery. The monster is galvanized into life in splendidly effective scenes—by harnessing electricity from lightning in the first film and through a generator (800° Fahrenheit, we are told) in the second, and Frankenstein is vulgarized from Shelley's idealistic and guilt-ridden scientist into an eccentric one getting crazier by the minute. The monster, in the first film of this series, was given a criminal's brain, and this is naïvely supposed to explain his evil nature from the start—Mary Shelley's socialistic message, of course, does not survive.

Bram Stoker's novel *Dracula* and later Gothic works were inspired by the much greater writer Sheridan Le Fanu, a point that needs emphasizing as the enormous success of Stoker's book has eclipsed his fellow Irishman. Stoker receives more attention because it is his image of the vampire—the tall pale Count in the black cloak, repeated and imitated in many books and films—that has become the standard image and immediately comes to mind. Apart from that, he is extremely readable.

The striking, convincing patterns made by the logical system of beliefs deriving from the vampire legend and the vividness of the symbols make 'suspension of disbelief' easy, and this explains the vast army of vampire-buffs. The films have eminently cinematic attributes to play with: the vampire's need to operate between sunset and sunrise; the graves and coffins; his ability to travel as motes of dust or wisps of fog, and change himself into a wolf, rat, bat and some other animals (which often accompany him and which he can control); his superhuman strength and hypnotic power; his aversion to crucifixes, garlic and wolfbane; his lack of reflection in a mirror; and the means of his destruction (a stake through the heart, after which decapitation and burning the corpse are extra precautions).

The first and greatly influential Dracula film was Murnau's *Nosferatu*, made in Germany in 1922, in which the vampire was played by Max Von Schrek. In 1931 the Hollywood version, *Dracula*, by Universal, with Bela Lugosi as Dracula, launched the whole series of horror films, including the various sequels on the Dracula theme as well as on the Frankenstein one. One or two of the earliest are regarded as classics and have been repeated on TV. In the 1960s Hammer Films of Great Britain returned to these and related themes—mummies, werewolves, zombies, and a number of 'creepies' adapted from Poe. There have been half a dozen excellent film versions of *Dr Jekyll and Mr Hyde* and three of Conan Doyle's *The Hound of the Baskervilles*, the most recent for television in 1974.

The best horror films, like the best Gothic literature, give shocking scenes a dramatic function and do not include them for mere sensation, and most have been adapted from novels worth attention. Again, as in literature, suggestiveness—albeit visual rather than verbal—often has a more powerful effect than explicitness.

Psychopathic disorder has been a common motif in recent horror films. Usually it is associated with sexual repression and family tensions. *Psycho*, from the novel by Robert Bloch, published in 1959, is a good example, and the nearest to a Gothic horror film made by one of the masters of cinematic suspense, Alfred Hitchcock. This film achieved some of the most spine-chilling effects seen in the cinema with very little violent action. A famous scene is that of the stabbing to death of a woman while under a shower, behind a shower curtain, in which almost everything is left to the imagination while the blood is seen trickling away with the bathwater.

The central character of *Psycho* is a schizophrenic who hates his mother, and the film inspired a number of 'schizophrenic' films, including *Homicidal*, *Blood Sisters* and *Schizo*. The threat to the family can, of course, be traced back to many different literary themes in the past; it is sufficient for the moment to trace it to *Frankenstein* and *Dracula* and their progeny. In some films the tensions are exteriorized and symbolized by violent upheavals in natural forces. In Hitchcock's *The Birds* (1963), from a story by Daphne du Maurier, when birds in thousands amass and terrorize a small town with sudden, ferocious invasions the horror comes from realizing how vulnerable and artificial are the family's barriers against disintegration. The forces for destruction may be slumbering within the institution—they are easily awakened, and turned against the institution itself. At the same time, the wider-spread tensions of a civilized society may find outlet in the destruction of natural forces and, as in *The Birds*, these may take revenge.

Satanism, backed up by varying degrees of occult lore, has been the direction taken by horror novels and films in the past year or two, and in the most striking examples the horror has been all the more suggestive and insidious by having the family background apparently innocently happy, bourgeois and well-ordered. In Roman Polanski's *Rosemary's Baby* (1968), from the novel by Ira Levin, the eponymous wife gives birth to an Antichrist with a cloven hoof, fathered by the Devil, and accepts the fact. In *The Exorcist* from William Peter Blatty's novel (1973), the young, well-balanced daughter Regan is suddenly possessed, the furniture hurled all over her bedroom, she emits obscenities and curses and vomits green bile (the film is in colour). All is restored to normality after some exorcism rites ending in a violent death.

The Omen (1976), film and novel by David Seltzer, is about an American ambassador to London and his wife, who have a demon-child, agent of the Devil's scheme to bring about the end of the world. The voice of reason is represented by a photographer who gets his head sawn off, and there is other violence and much occult business involving crucifixes. There are cheap effects in these films, but they have a flair and vitality to compensate.

The Gothic-horror films and the hybrid forms generated by combination with science fiction or with the occult, have a strong association with dreams, of the kind that inspired Walpole, Beckford and Mary Shelley. So we have not travelled too far away from our original trinity after all.

X. CONCLUSION

Much of the content of Gothic literature was inspired by dreams, or hallucinatory states that were self-induced or produced by drugs. The frequency of films based on Gothic literature is no accident—dreams are full of weird and vivid imagery that films can effectively present. Apart from that, both Gothic literature and Gothic-horror films, aiming to be popular (even when also aiming at art), are collective dreams, expressions of and safety-valves for the unconscious of the age, expressions of generally experienced desires and fears that tend to be repressed by individuals. This is part of the reason why the Gothic spirit is so easily given different forms in different ages.

This essay has had two principal aims. The first has been to show that a literary genre too often dismissed as being of little merit, as being a freak which disappeared into a cul-de-sac, can be seen when considered in a broader light as very important, as being the produce of a spirit that had antecedents in much great literature from ancient times, a spirit that was an essential part of Romanticism, a spirit, moreover, that far from dying out, divided itself and became the force behind other genres—notably supernatural fiction, detective fiction, thrillers and science fiction.

The second aim has been to point out that although a vast amount of what I have called 'Gothic literature'—all the literature that has a Gothic spirit and contains traces of direct influence from the Gothic novel of 1765–1820—is 'popular' literature and was intended primarily as escapist entertainment, nevertheless there are some greater writers and some very good ones who deserve attention and do not get it, because a false distinction tends to be made nowadays between 'good' and 'popular'. Shakespeare and Dickens were both, and so is Graham Greene. Perhaps Poe—in Britain at least—and Sheridan Le Fanu are the greatest of the writers neglected because they were, and are, taken to be narrower than they are. Matthew Lewis, Bram Stoker and H. P. Lovecraft are examples of writers who continue to be read, and deserve to be. Although they have faults, including awkward styles and a naïveté that produces unconscious humour, they nevertheless have more interest, more vitality and readableness, much less pretentiousness and altogether more value than many a ponderous literary 'classic' more honoured in the histories of literature than by any significant number of readers.

An occupational hazard of the literary critic is to play the association game—to follow the trails suggested by the various aspects of his subject so as to give those aspects greater significance. The problem is that when he comes to the end of the game he may find that he has arrived at a nebulous 'universal significance' and has lost sight of where he started from.

I have tried to avoid that by staying close to the theme. But here it might be useful to give a little more emphasis to a few of the fascinating trails the student of the Gothic might be tempted to follow up.

A compulsive interest in corpses and other manifestations of death, in demonstrating man's desire for immortality and fear of it, in developing understanding for the outcast, in analysing erotic sensibility and the effects of sexual repression, in exploring sado-masochism—these are prominent among the concerns of the Gothic novel.

The interest in, and often obsession with, the paraphernalia of death is obvious enough, with its medieval associations and the various antecedents in medieval literature. Mention has already been made of how an attitude of anti-rationalism encouraged these interests. The rattle of skeletons and the hollow stare of skulls pursue us from Walpole's castle to Frankenstein's laboratory, and through hundreds of abbeys and cloisters. It is the mixed desire and fear of immortality behind this, expressed in Frankenstein's monster and in the various treatments of Faust, the various representations of the Wandering Jew and the vampire and combinations of these figures, that demand to be explored. Christopher Marlowe based his play *The Tragical History of Dr Faustus*, first performed in the 1590s, on a popular tale published in 1587 by Johann Spies, who brought in the idea of Faust's selling his soul to the Devil in exchange for immortality; the character was based on a real Dr (Georg) Faust (1480–1540), an eccentric magician. Goethe's

Faust, the most famous, appeared in 1808 (Part I) and Thomas Mann's philosophical novel *Doktor Faustus* in 1947. In 1967 Marlowe's play was filmed as *Doctor Faustus* with Richard Burton and Elizabeth Taylor. There are many other versions to be explored and compared.

The original Wandering Jew was Cartophilus, Pontius Pilate's doorkeeper, who according to the legend struck Jesus Christ and told him to hurry. Christ replied, 'I am going, but you must wait until I come again'. Ever since, Cartophilus lives, every hundred years finding himself renewed as a 30-year-old. *Melmoth the Wanderer* is the best known of all developments of the legend, and like many other versions combines it with the Faustian theme.

Longings for immortality, the shape which man's spiritual desires tend to take, accompany in the Christian world fantasies about the Devil, and the Devil or his agent, in the different forms he has assumed in Gothic literature— whether a Byronic Fatal Hero, an immortal wanderer, a Faustian figure or a vampire, tends to be a romanticized image of freedom and power—in our dreams and in the Gothic novels this figure acts as we do not dare to act, lives as we do not dare to live, enjoys and suffers as we do not dare to: he represents our repressions.

Perhaps most conspicuously, our sexual repressions. Freud painted a picture of a Western civilization which had a dangerous quantity of sexual energy repressed by the institutions of the monogamous family. The Rochester of Charlotte Brontë's *Jane Eyre* and the Heathcliff of Emily Brontë's *Wuthering Heights* were fantasized outlets for this energy in the form of fiercely proud, anti-social, sexually dominating figures that towered over the other characters and were models for countless 'romantic' heroes, mainly of women writers, to come. Of the Gothic litany the vampire in the form of Bram Stoker's Count Dracula is most obviously another manifestation of that outlet. The common love bite is, after all, aimed at the jugular vein, like the vampire's, and the eroticism of vampire novels is mainly disguised, implicit, symbolical, as it is in the Brontës.

Stakes penetrating the heart, the gushing of blood, and much other Gothic-horror imagery in both films and novels were exploited for their erotic overtones when sexual explicitness was banned. Now that censorship is much laxer, the fact that there is little need for such disguise may be one reason why the traditional Gothic-horror themes have tended in recent years to give way to the more suggestive psychological and occult themes. The demon-child that has appeared in several recent films is significant as a Freudian symbol, representing the repressed energies of the civilized family.

Mention has been made in chapter VIII of Mario Praz's survey of the manifestations of erotic sensibility, including algolagnia, in the Romantic literature of three languages. The last two paragraphs above may suggest ways in which Praz's theme might be explored further.

Finally, Frankenstein's monster, Radcliffe and Lewis's pale monks, Melmoth, the suffering outcasts of Poe and all the other Gothic hero-villains or anti-heroes that compel our attention and sympathy (even if also our condemnation), have strong links with the 'outsiders' in the novels of some of the greatest European writers of this century—Kafka, Camus, Sartre, Beckett and others.

The perpetual attraction of the tale of terror, H. P. Lovecraft said, was 'the scratching of unknown claws at the rind of the known world'. That is certainly what you hear in the best of the Gothic novels, and when you hear it in the passages of the great writers that have forced their way into this essay, the sound, however intermittent, is unmistakable and unforgettable.

THE GOTHIC NOVEL
A Select Bibliography
(Place of publication London, unless stated otherwise)

Bibliographies

GEMMETT, ROBERT J: *An Annotated Checklist of the Works of William Beckford:* Papers of the Bibliographical Society of America, 3rd Quarter, LXI, pp 143–58 (1967).

HAZEN, A T: *A Bibliography of Horace Walpole*, Yale University Press, New Haven (1948).

SUMMERS, MONTAGUE: *A Gothic Bibliography*, Fortune Press (1940).

WISE, T J: *A Shelley Library*. Catalogues, printed books, MSS, and autograph letters (1924).

The Gothic Genre

BECKFORD, W T: *Vathek*, ed. R Lonsdale. Oxford English Novels Series, OUP (1965).

GODWIN, WILLIAM: *The Adventures of Caleb Williams, or, Things as they are*. Introduction by G Sherburn. Rinehart & Co, New York, Toronto (1960).

LEWIS, MATTHEW G: *The Monk*. Introduction by J Berryman, Grove Press, New York (1952).

MATURIN, CHARLES: *Melmoth the Wanderer*. Introduction by A Hayter. Penguin (1977).

RADCLIFFE, ANN: *The Mysteries of Udolpho*, ed. B Dobrée, OUP (1966). *The Italian*, ed. F Garber, Oxford English Novels Series, OUP (1968).

REEVE, CLARA: (*The Champion of Virtue*). Retitled *The Old English Baron. A Gothic Story*, ed. J Trainer, OUP (1967).

SHELLEY, MARY: *Frankenstein, or, The Modern Prometheus*, ed. M K Joseph, Oxford English Novels Series, OUP (1971).

WALPOLE, BECKFORD; MARY SHELLEY: *Three Gothic Novels: The Castle of Otranto, Vathek* and *Frankenstein*, ed. P Fairclough. Introduction by M Praz. Penguin English Library Series (1968).

WALPOLE, HORACE: *The Castle of Otranto*. Introduction by Sir Walter Scott. Preface by C F E Spurgeon. Chatto (1907).

Gothic-Related Fiction

ALDISS, BRIAN: *Frankenstein Unbound*, Cape (1973).

AUSTEN, JANE: *Northanger Abbey*. Introduction by A H Ehrenpreis, Penguin (1972).

BALZAC, HONORÉ DE: *The Wild Ass's Skin*. Translated by H Hunt, Penguin (1977).

BLATTY, WILLIAM PETER: *The Exorcist*, Blond & Briggs (1971). Originally published by Harper and Row, New York (1971).

BRONTË, CHARLOTTE: *Jane Eyre*, Penguin (1971).
BRONTË, EMILY: *Wuthering Heights*, ed. D Daiches, Penguin (1965).
CARTER, ANGELA: *Shadow Dance. The Magic Toyshop*, Heinemann (1966), (1967). *The Infernal Desire Machine of Dr Hoffman*, Hart-Davis (1972).
BULWER-LYTTON, LORD: *The Haunted and the Haunters, or, The House and the Brain*, Gowan's International Library No 1, London, Glasgow (1905).
COLLINS, WILKIE: *The Moonstone. The Woman in White*, Everyman's Library Series, Dent (1963), Penguin (1966), (1974).
DOYLE, ARTHUR CONAN: *The Hound of the Baskervilles*. Illustrated by S Hughes, Murray (1957).
DE LA MARE, WALTER: *Memoirs of a Midget*, Collins (1921). Republished by Penguin (1955).
GOGOL, NIKOLAI V: *The Diary of a Madman*. Translated by R Wilkes (contains *The Nose* and *The Overcoat*), Penguin (1972): *Tales of Good and Evil*. Translated by D Magarshack. (contains *The Portrait*), Lehmann (1949).
HAWTHORNE, NATHANIEL: *The House of the Seven Gables*, Harper & Row, New York (1965).
HOFFMANN, E T: *The Devil's Elixir*. Translated by R Taylor. Illustrated by H Weissenborn, Calder & Boyars (1963). *Tales of Hoffmann*. Translated by J Kirkup, London and Glasgow (1966).
JAMES, HENRY: *The Turn of the Screw*, Penguin (1946).
KAFKA, FRANZ: *The Castle*. Translated by W and E Muir, Penguin (1957). *Metamorphosis*, Penguin (1970). Penguin in association with Secker (1974).
LE FANU, SHERIDAN: *In a Glass Darkly*. Contains the stories 'Green Tea' and 'Carmilla'. Introduction by V S Pritchett, Lehmann (1947). *The House by the Churchyard*, Doughty Library Series, Blond (1968). *Uncle Silas*, Dover Publications (1968).
LOVECRAFT, H P: *The Haunter of the Dark, and other tales of horror*, ed. A Dereoth, Gollancz (1951).
MURDOCH, IRIS: *The Unicorn. The Time of the Angels*, Penguin (1971).
PEACOCK, THOMAS LOVE: *Nightmare Abbey* (with *Crotchet Castle*). Introduction by R Wright, Penguin (1976).
POE, EDGAR ALLAN: *Selected Writings*, ed. D. Galloway, Penguin (1976).
PUSHKIN, ALEXANDER S: *The Queen of Spades*, ed. R Edmonds, Penguin (1962).
SARTRE, JEAN-PAUL: (*Les Autres*) retitled *Huis Clos*. Translated as *No Exit* by P Bowles. A one-act play, Samuel French, New York (1958).
SELTZER, DAVID: *The Omen*, Barker (1976).
STEVENSON, ROBERT LOUIS: *The Strange Case of Dr Jekyll and Mr Hyde, and other Macabre Stories* (by other authors), Transworld Publishers (Corgi Books) (1974).
STOKER, BRAM: *Dracula*, Jarrolds (1966).
SUMMERS, MONTAGUE: *The Supernatural Omnibus*, Gollancz (1931).

WILDE, OSCAR: *The Picture of Dorian Gray*. With illustrations by H Keen, John Lane; Dodd, Mead & Co, New York (1925).

Works of Criticism

ASHLEY, MIKE: *Who's Who in Horror and Fantasy Fiction*, Elm Tree Books/Hamish Hamilton (1977).

BATAILLE, GEORGES: *Literature and Evil (La Littérature et le mal)*. Translated by A Hamilton, Calder & Boyars (1973).

BIRKHEAD, EDITH: *The Tale of Terror*. A Study of Gothic Romance, Constable (1921).

CAMUS, ALBERT: *The Rebel*, Penguin (1974). Contains a chapter, 'Byronic Outsiders'.

CLARK, KENNETH: *The Gothic Revival*, Murray (1928). Latest edition 1974.

DE QUINCEY, THOMAS: *Confessions of an English Opium-Eater*, ed. and with an introduction by A Hayter, Penguin (1971).

HAYTER, ALETHEA: *Opium and the Romantic Imagination*, Faber (1968).

HONOUR, HUGH: *Horace Walpole* (Writers and Their Work Series), Longman (1957). Revised edition 1970.

JAMES, LOUIS: *Fiction for the Working Man, 1830-50*. A study of the literature produced for the Working Classes in Early Victorian Urban England, OUP (1963).

KETTON-CREMER, R W: *Horace Walpole*. A biography, Methuen (1940). Cornell University Press (1966).

LOVECRAFT, H P: *Supernatural Horror in Literature, etc.*, Ben Abramson, New York (1945).

Oxford History of English Literature, eds. F P Wilson and B Dobree. Vol IX: 1789-1815 by W L Renwick; Vol X: 1915-32 by I Jack.

PRAZ, MARIO: *The Romantic Agony*, OUP (1933). 2nd edition with new foreword by F Kermode, 1970.

RAILO, EINO: *The Haunted Castle*. A Study of the Elements of English Romanticism, Routledge (1927).

SMITH, WARREN HUNTING: (ed.) *Horace Walpole: Writer, Politician and Connoisseur:* Essays on the 250th Anniversary of Walpole's Death, Yale University Press, New Haven and London (1967).

SPARK, MURIEL: *Child of Light: A Reassessment of Mary Wollstonecraft Shelley*, Tower Bridge Publications, Hadleigh (1951).

STUART, DOROTHY M: *Horace Walpole*, Macmillan (1927).

SUMMERS, MONTAGUE: *The Gothic Quest. A History of the Gothic Novel*, Fortune Press (1938). *The Vampire: his Kith and Kin* (with a bibliography), Kegan Paul (1929). *The Werewolf* (with Plates and a bibliography), Kegan Paul (1933).

TOMPKINS, J M S: *The Popular Novel in England, 1770-1800*, Constable (1932) reprinted by Methuen (1962).

VARMA, DEVENDRA P: *The Gothic Flame*. Foreword by H Read. Introduction by J M S Tompkins, Barker (1957).

WILLEY, BASIL: *The 18th Century Background*. Studies on the idea of Nature in the thought of the period, Penguin in association with Chatto (1962). Originally published by Chatto (1940). *Nineteenth Century Studies. Coleridge to Matthew Arnold*, Chatto (1949).

Shorter Essays and Articles

CRUDE, WILFRED: 'Mary Shelley's Modern Prometheus: A Study in the Ethics of Scientific Creativity'. Dalhousie Review, LII, pp 812–25 (1972).

FOLSOM, J K: 'Beckford's Vathek and the Tradition of Oriental Satire'. *Criticism*, VI (1964).

GRAHAM, KENNETH W: 'Beckford's Vathek: A Study in Ironic Dissonance'. Criticism XIV, pp 243–52 (1972).

HUME, ROBERT D: 'Gothic versus Romantic: A Revaluation of the Gothic Novel'. PMLA, LXXXIV, pp 282–90 (March, 1969).

SADLEIR, MICHAEL: 'The Northanger Novels—A Footnote to Jane Austen'. Oxford (1927). English Association Pamphlet (1968).

WOOD, ROBIN: 'Return of the repressed'. (On the implications of the horror film). *Times Educational Supplement* (31 December 1976).

WRITERS AND THEIR WORK

SHERIDAN: W. A. Darlington
SMART: Geoffrey Grigson
SMOLLETT: Laurence Brander
STEELE, ADDISON: A. R. Humphreys
STERNE: D. W. Jefferson
SWIFT: J. Middleton Murry (1955)
SWIFT: A. Norman Jeffares (1976)
VANBRUGH: Bernard Harris
HORACE WALPOLE: Hugh Honour

Nineteenth Century:
ARNOLD: Kenneth Allott
AUSTEN: S. Townsend Warner (1951)
AUSTEN: B. C. Southam (1975)
BAGEHOT: N. St John-Stevas
THE BRONTË SISTERS:
                    Phyllis Bentley (1950)
THE BRONTËS: I & II: Winifred Gérin
E. B. BROWNING: Alethea Hayter
ROBERT BROWNING: John Bryson
SAMUEL BUTLER: G. D. H. Cole
BYRON: I, II & III: Bernard Blackstone
CARLYLE: David Gascoyne (1952)
CARLYLE: Ian Campbell (1978)
CARROLL: Derek Hudson
CLOUGH: Isobel Armstrong
COLERIDGE: Kathleen Raine
CREEVEY & GREVILLE: J. Richardson
DE QUINCEY: Hugh Sykes Davies
DICKENS: K. J. Fielding
    EARLY NOVELS: T. Blount
    LATER NOVELS: B. Hardy
DISRAELI: Paul Bloomfield
GEORGE ELIOT: Lettice Cooper
FITZGERALD: Joanna Richardson
GASKELL: Miriam Allott
GISSING: A. C. Ward
HARDY: R. A. Scott-James
                    and C. Day Lewis
HAZLITT: J. B. Priestley (1960)
HAZLITT: R. L. Brett (1977)
HOOD: Laurence Brander
HOPKINS: Geoffrey Grigson
T. H. HUXLEY: William Irvine
KEATS: Edmund Blunden (1950)
KEATS: Miriam Allott (1976)
LAMB: Edmund Blunden
LANDOR: G. Rostrevor Hamilton

LEAR: Joanna Richardson
MACAULAY: G. R. Potter (1959)
MACAULAY: Kenneth Young (1976)
MEREDITH: Phyllis Bartlett
MILL: Maurice Cranston
MORRIS: P. Henderson
NEWMAN: J. M. Cameron
PATER: Ian Fletcher
PEACOCK: J. I. M. Stewart
CHRISTINA ROSSETTI: G. Battiscombe
D. G. ROSSETTI: Oswald Doughty
RUSKIN: Peter Quennell
SCOTT: Ian Jack
SHELLEY: G. M. Matthews
SOUTHEY: Geoffrey Carnall
STEPHEN: Phyllis Grosskurth
STEVENSON: G. B. Stern
SWINBURNE: Ian Fletcher
TENNYSON: B. C. Southam
THACKERAY: Laurence Brander
FRANCIS THOMPSON: P. Butter
TROLLOPE: Hugh Sykes Davies
WILDE: James Laver
WORDSWORTH: Helen Darbishire

Twentieth Century:
ACHEBE: A. Ravenscroft
ARDEN: Glenda Leeming
AUDEN: Richard Hoggart
BECKETT: J-J. Mayoux
BELLOC: Renée Haynes
BENNETT: Frank Swinnerton (1950)
BENNETT: Kenneth Young (1975)
BETJEMAN: John Press
BLUNDEN: Alec M. Hardie
BOND: Simon Trussler
BRIDGES: J. Sparrow
BURGESS: Carol M. Dix
CAMPBELL: David Wright
CARY: Walter Allen
CHESTERTON: C. Hollis
CHURCHILL: John Connell
COLLINGWOOD: E. W. F. Tomlin
COMPTON-BURNETT: R. Glynn Grylls
CONRAD: Oliver Warner (1950)
CONRAD: C. B. Cox (1977)
DE LA MARE: Kenneth Hopkins
NORMAN DOUGLAS: Ian Greenlees

LAWRENCE DURRELL: G. S. Fraser
T. S. ELIOT: M. C. Bradbrook
T. S. ELIOT: The Making of
'The Waste Land': M. C. Bradbrook
FORD MADOX FORD: Kenneth Young
FORSTER: Rex Warner (1950)
FORSTER: Philip Gardener
FRY: Derek Stanford
GALSWORTHY: R. H. Mottram
GOLDING: Stephen Medcalf
GRAVES: M. Seymour-Smith
GRAHAM GREENE: Francis Wyndham
HARTLEY: Paul Bloomfield
A. E. HOUSMAN: Ian Scott-Kilvert
TED HUGHES: Keith Sagar
ALDOUS HUXLEY: Jocelyn Brooke
ISHERWOOD: Francis King
HENRY JAMES: Michael Swan
HANSFORD JOHNSON: Isabel Quigly
JOYCE: J. I. M. Stewart
KIPLING: Bonamy Dobrée
LARKIN: Alan Brownjohn
D. H. LAWRENCE:
              Kenneth Young (1952)
D. H. LAWRENCE: I:
              J. C. F. Littlewood (1976)
LESSING: Michael Thorpe
C. DAY LEWIS: Clifford Dyment
WYNDHAM LEWIS: E. W. F. Tomlin
MACDIARMID: Edwin Morgan
MACKENZIE: Kenneth Young
MACNEICE: John Press
MANSFIELD: Ian Gordon
MASEFIELD: L. A. G. Strong
MAUGHAM: J. Brophy
GEORGE MOORE: A. Norman Jeffares

MURDOCH: A. S. Byatt
NAIPAUL: Michael Thorpe
NARAYAN: William Walsh
NEWBY: G. S. Fraser
O'CASEY: W. A. Armstrong
ORWELL: Tom Hopkinson
OSBORNE: Simon Trussler
OWEN: Dominic Hibberd
PINTER: John Russell Taylor
POETS OF THE 1939-45 WAR:
              R. N. Currey
POWELL: Bernard Bergonzi
POWYS BROTHERS: R. C. Churchill
PRIESTLEY: Ivor Brown (1957)
PRIESTLEY: Kenneth Young (1977)
PROSE WRITERS OF WORLD WAR I:
              M. S. Greicus
HERBERT READ: Francis Berry
SHAFFER: John Russell Taylor
SHAW: A. C. Ward
EDITH SITWELL: John Lehmann
SNOW: William Cooper
SPARK: Patricia Stubbs
STOPPARD: C. W. E. Bigsby
STOREY: John Russell Taylor
SYNGE & LADY GREGORY: E. Coxhead
DYLAN THOMAS: G. S. Fraser
G. M. TREVELYAN: J. H. Plumb
WAR POETS: 1914-18: E. Blunden
EVELYN WAUGH: Christopher Hollis
WELLS: Kenneth Young
WESKER: Glenda Leeming
PATRICK WHITE: R. F. Brissenden
ANGUS WILSON: K. W. Gransden
VIRGINIA WOOLF: B. Blackstone
YEATS: G. S. Fraser

Shakespeare
the writer and his work

A WRITERS AND THEIR WORK SPECIAL

by Stanley Wells

The *Writers and Their Work* series already contains ten essays by different contributors on the subject of Shakespeare's life, and the various categories of the plays and poems, each equipped with a separate bibliography. This specially commissioned booklet offers the reader a compendious and attractively illustrated survey of the complete works, together with a single select bibliography.

Following a biographical chapter and a sketch of the English drama and theatre of Shakespeare's time, the main body of the essay offers a scholarly account and a critical survey of the plays and poems. Shakespeare's writings are divided into four sections, those composed before 1594, 1594–1600, 1600–1607, and 1607–1612: the plays within these divisions are grouped by genre. Dr Wells' appreciation combines a keen awareness of the literary and poetic qualities of the plays with an understanding of their theatrical effectiveness. The final chapters review the publication and editing of Shakespeare's works, their theatrical history, and the development of Shakespearean criticism over the past four centuries.

Dr Wells is General Editor of the Oxford Shakespeare (in preparation), and Head of the Shakespeare Department at the Oxford University Press. From 1962–1977 he was a Fellow of the Shakespeare Institute of the University of Birmingham with special responsibility for the Institute's activities in Stratford-upon-Avon where he lived. He has edited three of Shakespeare's plays in the *New Penguin* series and has published extensively on Shakespeare and his contemporaries. From 1980 he will be the editor of *Shakespeare Survey*, the leading annual journal of Shakespeare studies in Britain.

LONGMAN FOR THE BRITISH COUNCIL